TENNYSON

Compiled and Illustrated
by
Patricia Machin

Grange BOOKS

Published by Grange Books
An Imprint of Books & Toys Limited
The Grange
Grange Yard
LONDON SE1 3AG
ISBN 1 85627 255 9

This edition published 1992

First published in Great Britain 1985 by
Webb & Bower (Publishers) Limited
9 Colleton Crescent, Exeter, Devon EX2 4BY

Typeset in Great Britain by P&M Typesetting Limited,
Exeter, Devon

Printed in Spain by
Gráficas Reunidas, S. A.

Contents

Introduction

Alfred Tennyson was the third son of George and Elizabeth Tennyson; he had six brothers and four sisters. George Tennyson had been disinherited by his father in favour of a younger son, Charles; his father then arranged for him to take Holy Orders and secured him the living at Somersby in Lincolnshire, not far from the family estate at Bayons. He had no vocation for the Church and it was to be a continual grievance to him that he was not to inherit his father's wealth and estate.

The Rectory at Somersby was too small for George Tennyson's large family who were brought up in humbler circumstances than their cousins at Bayons. They were educated mainly at home by their father, who, although a rather unstable character and unable to come to terms with his disinheritance, was a scholar with wide interests and a good library.

There can be no doubt that the poet's early years — the freedom from conventional schooling and the encouragement and scholarship received from his father — greatly contributed to his development. Nevertheless, home life at the Rectory, involving the children in their father's bitterness and humiliation, and the horror of his eventual breakdown and alcoholism, deeply and tragically affected the whole family and made a lasting impression on Alfred.

Tennyson was highly esteemed, even idolized during his life-time but neglected for many years after his death, when there was a reaction against all things Victorian.

It is not difficult for us to understand what an unsettling period this must have been, with the discoveries and progress of science coming so rapidly and challenging everything that had been taken as the permanent truth relating to God and man, life and death; Tennyson, far from escaping into a private world of poetry, was immensely concerned with these changes and the effect they had on people.

This deep concern was reflected in his poetry throughout his life and has always endeared him to his readers; it ranks him among the most human of the great poets.

The romance of medieval castles captured the imagination of the Victorians and represented for them a fairy-tale world far removed from the grim industrial development that was taking over their lives so rapidly. During this period the wealthy built enormous and fanciful 'castles'. Tennyson's cousins built just such a castle at Bayons but it became an abandoned ruin within a hundred years. It is interesting to reflect that the name Tennyson is remembered through the poet and not through this great display of wealth so soon to pass away.

The Splendour Falls

The splendour falls on castle walls
    And snowy summits old in story;
The long light shakes across the lakes,
    And the wild cataract leaps in glory.
Blow, bugle, blow, set the wild echoes flying,
Blow, bugle; answer, echoes, dying, dying, dying.

O hark, O hear! how thin and clear,
    And thinner, clearer, farther going!
O sweet and far from cliff and scar
    The horns of Elfland faintly blowing!
Blow, let us hear the purple glens replying:
Blow, bugle; answer, echoes, dying, dying, dying.

O love, they die in yon rich sky,
    They faint on hill or field or river:
Our echoes roll from soul to soul,
    And grow for ever and for ever.
Blow, bugle, blow, set the wild echoes flying,
And answer, echoes, answer, dying, dying, dying.

This unique and powerful poem was included in *Poems Chiefly Lyrical* a volume that Tennyson published in 1830 when he was an undergraduate at Cambridge. A sea-monster of Scandinavian folk-lore, the Kraken is said to represent here the young poet's feelings of isolation and self-imprisonment and his eventual release through his own creative power. Tennyson's father died in 1831 and the poet was obliged to return to Somersby to look after the rest of his family without taking his degree. He had, however, won the Chancellor's Gold Medal for Poetry in 1829.

The Kraken

BELOW the thunders of the upper deep;
Far, far beneath in the abysmal sea,
His ancient, dreamless, uninvaded sleep
The Kraken sleepeth: faintest sunlights flee
About his shadowy sides: above him swell
Huge sponges of millennial growth and height;
And far away into the sickly light,
From many a wondrous grot and secret cell
Unnumber'd and enormous polyp:
Winnow with giant arms the slumbering green.
There hath he lain for ages and will lie
Battening upon huge seaworms in his sleep,
Until the latter fire shall heat the deep;
Then once by man and angels to be seen,
In roaring he shall rise and on the surface die.

This is a one of
a group of poems
Tennyson called his English
Idylls because they were
inspired by the classic works
of the Greek and Roman poets
in which he had been so
brilliantly instructed by his
father.

Three sections of this rather
long poem are illustrated here.
The narrator, an artist, is
introduced to the garden by
another artist and the poem,
with its ravishing descrip-
tions, is said to represent
the English language at its
most expressive.

The Gardener's Daughter;

OR, THE PICTURES

THIS morning is the morning of the day,
Not wholly in the busy world, nor quite
Beyond it, blooms the garden that I love.
News from the humming city comes to it
In sound of funeral or of marriage bells;
And, sitting muffled in dark leaves, you hear
The windy clanging of the minster clock;
Although between it and the garden lies
A league of grass, wash'd by a slow broad stream,
That, stirr'd with languid pulses of the oar,
Waves all its lazy lilies, and creeps on,
Barge-laden, to three arches of a bridge
Crown'd with the minster-towers.

                     The fields between
Are dewy-fresh, browsed by deep-udder'd kine,
And all about the large lime feathers low,
The lime a summer home of murmurous wings.
  In that still place she, hoarded in herself,
Grew, seldom seen; not less among us lived
Her fame from lip to lip. Who had not heard
Of Rose, the Gardener's daughter?

He cried, 'Look! look!' Before he ceased I turn'd,
And, ere a star can wink, beheld her there.
  For up the porch there grew an Eastern rose,
That, flowering high, the last night's gale had
                       caught,
And blown across the walk. One arm aloft–
Gown'd in pure white, that fitted to the shape–
Holding the bush, to fix it back, she stood,
A single stream of all her soft brown hair
Pour'd on one side: the shadow of the flowers
Stole all the golden gloss, and, wavering
Lovingly lower, trembled on her waist–
Ah, happy shade–and still went wavering
                   down,
But, ere it touch'd a foot, that might have
                   danced
The greensward into greener circles, dipt,
And mix'd with shadows of the common ground!

There sat we down upon a garden mound,
Two mutually enfolded; Love, the third,
Between us, in the circle of his arms
Enwound us both; and over many a range
Of waning lime the gray cathedral towers,
Across a hazy glimmer of the west,
Reveal'd their shining windows: from them
                                    clash'd
The bells; we listen'd; with the time we play'd,
We spoke of other things; we coursed about
The subject most at heart, more near and near,
Like doves about a dovecote, wheeling round
The central wish, until we settled there.
    Then, in that time and place, I spoke to
                                    her,
Requiring, tho' I knew it was mine own,
Yet for the pleasure that I took to hear,
Requiring at her hand the greatest gift,
A woman's heart, the heart of her I loved;

Three Poems
from 'The Princess'

Tennyson's interest in the social
issues of the day led him to write
The Princess a long poem which was
so well received and successful that
he was at last able to marry Emily
Selwood after a wait of ten years
due to financial insecurity. It is
written as a tale composed by some
young people sitting in a romantic
ruin on a summer's day. Each
contributes to the tale in turn and
the whole forms an exciting story
concerning the liberation of
women — a very modern theme for
those days.

Sweet and low, sweet and low,
  Wind of the western sea,
Low, low, breathe and blow,
  Wind of the western sea!
Over the rolling waters go,
Come from the dying moon, and blow,
  Blow him again to me;
While my little one, while my pretty one,
                              sleeps.

Sleep and rest, sleep and rest,
  Father will come to thee soon;
Rest, rest, on mother's breast,
  Father will come to thee soon;
Father will come to his babe in the nest,
Silver sails all out of the west
  Under the silver moon:
Sleep, my little one, sleep, my pretty
                              one, sleep.

As thro' the land at eve we went,
    And pluck'd the ripen'd ears,
We fell out, my wife and I,
O we fell out I know not why,
    And kiss'd again with tears.
And blessings on the falling out
    That all the more endears,
When we fall out with those we
                            love
    And kiss again with tears!
For when we came where lies the
                            child
    We lost in other years,
There above the little grave,
O there above the little grave,
    We kiss'd again with tears.

Home they brought her warrior dead:
   She nor swoon'd, nor utter'd cry:
All her maidens, watching, said,
'She must weep or she will die.'

Then they praised him, soft and low,
   Call'd him worthy to be loved,
Truest friend and noblest foe;
   Yet she neither spoke nor moved.

Stole a maiden from her place,
   Lightly to the warrior stept,
Took the face-cloth from the face;
   Yet she neither moved nor wept.

Rose a nurse of ninety years,
   Set his child upon her knee–
Like summer tempest came her tears–
   'Sweet my child, I live for thee.'

The legend of King Arthur and the Knights of the Round Table interested Tennyson for many years. He based his famous *Idylls of the King* on the story after studying the work of Sir Thomas Malory (d.1471). This poem, of which six verses are illustrated here, was in fact written before *The Idylls*, together with the poet's own version of Malory's *Mort d'Arthur*.

Sir Galahad represents the fervent devotion to an ideal so dear to the Victorians; his search was for the Holy Grail, the cup from which Jesus drank at the Last Supper. Galahad was the only knight to find it.

Sir Galahad

My good blade carves the casques of men,
  My tough lance thrusteth sure,
My strength is as the strength of ten,
  Because my heart is pure.
The shattering trumpet shrilleth high,
  The hard brands shiver on the steel,
The splinter'd spear-shafts crack and fly,
  The horse and rider reel:
They reel, they roll in clanging lists,
  And when the tide of combat stands,
Perfume and flowers fall in showers,
  That lightly rain from ladies' hands.

How sweet are looks that ladies bend
  On whom their favours fall!
For them I battle till the end,
  To save from shame and thrall:
But all my heart is drawn above,
  My knees are bow'd in crypt and shrine:
I never felt the kiss of love,
  Nor maiden's hand in mine.
More bounteous aspects on me beam,
  Me mightier transports move and thrill;
So keep I fair thro' faith and prayer
  A virgin heart in work and will.

When down the stormy crescent goes,
    A light before me swims,
Between dark stems the forest glows,
    I hear a noise of hymns:
Then by some secret shrine I ride;
    I hear a voice but none are there;
The stalls are void, the doors are wide,
    The tapers burning fair.
Fair gleams the snowy altar-cloth,
    The silver vessels sparkle clean,
The shrill bell rings, the censer swings,
    And solemn chaunts resound between.

Sometimes on lonely mountain-meres
    I find a magic bark;
I leap on board: no helmsman steers:
    I float till all is dark.
A gentle sound, an awful light!
    Three angels bear the holy Grail:
With folded feet, in stoles of white,
    On sleeping wings they sail.
Ah, blessed vision! blood of God!
    My spirit beats her mortal bars,
As down dark tides the glory slides,
    And star-like mingles with the stars.

When on my goodly charger borne
   Thro' dreaming towns I go,
The cock crows ere the Christmas morn,
   The streets are dumb with snow.
The tempest crackles on the leads,
   And, ringing, springs from brand and mail;
But o'er the dark a glory spreads,
   And gilds the driving hail.
I leave the plain, I climb the height;
   No branchy thicket shelter yields;
But blessed forms in whistling storms
   Fly o'er waste fens and windy fields.

The clouds are broken in the sky,
   And thro' the mountain-walls
A rolling organ-harmony
   Swells up, and shakes and falls.
Then move the trees, the copses nod,
   Wings flutter, voices hover clear:
'O just and faithful knight of God!
   Ride on! the prize is near.'
So pass I hostel, hall, and grange;
   By bridge and ford, by park and pale,
All-arm'd I ride, whate'er betide,
   Until I find the holy Grail.

It is well known that Tennyson wrote *In Memoriam*, a long elegaic poem, in his grief at the death of Arthur Hallum but it is not always realized that he wrote this poem for the same reason. Hallum, a brilliant Cambridge undergraduate, had been Tennyson's friend, mentor and critic at a time when the young poet most needed help to overcome the family affliction of black melancholia which often weighed upon him. Arthur Hallum, who became engaged to one of the poet's sisters, completely filled this role until his death at the age of twenty-one.

BREAK, break, break,
  On thy cold gray stones, O Sea!
And I would that my tongue could utter
  The thoughts that arise in me.

O well for the fisherman's boy,
  That he shouts with his sister at play!
O well for the sailor lad,
  That he sings in his boat on the bay!

And the stately ships go on
  To their haven under the hill;
But O for the touch of a vanish'd hand,
  And the sound of a voice that is still!

Break, break, break,
  At the foot of thy crags, O Sea!
But the tender grace of a day that is dead
  Will never come back to me.

Tennyson must have derived much pleasure from observing nature from the days of his childhood in the Lincolnshire Wolds throughout his life, for he describes so succintly and with such artistry the characteristics of the birds in these three poems as in many others.

The great technical skill and originality of these three poems is deceptive, for they are simple enough for very small children to understand and enjoy.

The Blackbird

O BLACKBIRD! sing me something well:
  While all the neighbours shoot thee round,
  I keep smooth plats of fruitful ground,
Where thou may'st warble, eat and dwell.

The espaliers and the standards all
  Are thine; the range of lawn and park:
  The unnetted black-hearts ripen dark,
All thine, against the garden wall.

Yet, tho' I spared thee all the spring,
  Thy sole delight is, sitting still,
  With that gold dagger of thy bill
To fret the summer jenneting.

A golden bill! the silver tongue,
  Cold February loved, is dry:
  Plenty corrupts the melody
That made thee famous once, when young:

And in the sultry garden-squares,
  Now thy flute-notes are changed to coarse,
  I hear thee not at all, or hoarse
As when a hawker hawks his wares.

Take warning! he that will not sing
  While yon sun prospers in the blue,
  Shall sing for want, ere leaves are new,
Caught in the frozen palms of Spring.

The Throstle

'SUMMER is coming, summer is coming.
  I know it, I know it, I know it.
Light again, leaf again, life again, love again.'
  Yes, my wild little Poet.

Sing the new year in under the blue.
  Last year you sang it as gladly.
'New, new, new, new'! Is it then so new
  That you should carol so madly?

'Love again, song again, nest again, young again,'
  Never a prophet so crazy!
And hardly a daisy as yet, little friend,
  See, there is hardly a daisy.

'Here again, here, here, here, happy year'!
  O warble unchidden, unbidden!
Summer is coming, is coming, my dear,
  And all the winters are hidden.

The Eagle

He clasps the crag with crooked hands;
Close to the sun in lonely lands,
Ring'd with the azure world, he stands.

The wrinkled sea beneath him crawls;
He watches from his mountain walls,
And like a thunderbolt he falls.

At the time this poem was written churchyard scenes were a very popular subject — people seemed more pre-occupied with bereavement and death than they are today. The Pre-Raphaelite Brotherhood, a group of painters working at that time with singular artistry and conviction, also used the graveyard and its mourning visitors as subject matter. Their pictures became unfashionable in the first part of the present century but are now very highly valued.

Edward Gray

SWEET Emma Moreland of yonder town
    Met me walking on yonder way,
'And have you lost your heart?' she said;
    'And are you married yet, Edward Gray?'

Sweet Emma Moreland spoke to me:
    Bitterly weeping I turn'd away:
'Sweet Emma Moreland, love no more
    Can touch the heart of Edward Gray.

'Ellen Adair she loved me well,
    Against her father's and mother's will:
To-day I sat for an hour and wept,
    By Ellen's grave, on the windy hill.

'Shy she was, and I thought her cold;
    Thought her proud, and fled over the sea;
Fill'd I was with folly and spite,
    When Ellen Adair was dying for me.

'Cruel, cruel the words I said!
    Cruelly came they back to-day:
"You're too slight and fickle," I said,
    "To trouble the heart of Edward Gray."

'There I put my face in the grass–
    Whisper'd, "Listen to my despair:
I repent me of all I did:
    Speak a little, Ellen Adair!"

'Then I took a pencil, and wrote
    On the mossy stone, as I lay,
"Here lies the body of Ellen Adair;
    And here the heart of Edward Gray!"

'Love may come, and love may go,
And fly, like a bird, from tree to tree;
But I will love no more, no more,
    Till Ellen Adair come back to me.

'Bitterly wept I over the stone:
    Bitterly weeping I turn'd away:
There lies the body of Ellen Adair!
    And there the heart of Edward Gray!'

Maud

Come into the garden, Maud,
   For the black bat, night, has flown,
Come into the garden, Maud,
   I am here at the gate alone;
And the woodbine spices are wafted abroad,
   And the musk of the rose is blown.

For a breeze of morning moves,
   And the planet of Love is on high,
Beginning to faint in the light that she loves
   On a bed of daffodil sky,
To faint in the light of the sun she loves,
   To faint in his light, and to die.

All night have the roses heard
   The flute, violin, bassoon;
All night has the casement jessamine stirr'd
   To the dancers dancing in tune;
Till a silence fell with the waking bird,
   And a hush with the setting moon.

I said to the lily, 'There is but one
   With whom she has heart to be gay.
When will the dancers leave her alone?
   She is weary of dance and play.'
Now half to the setting moon are gone,
   And half to the rising day;
Low on the sand and loud on the stone
   The last wheel echoes away.

I said to the rose, 'The brief night goes
   In babble and revel and wine.
O young lord-lover, what sighs are those,
   For one that will never be thine?
But mine, but mine,' so I sware to the rose,
'For ever and ever, mine.'

And the soul of the rose went into my blood,
   As the music clash'd in the hall;
And long by the garden lake I stood,
   For I heard your rivulet fall
From the lake to the meadow and on to the wood,
   Our wood, that is dearer than all;

From the meadow your walks have left so sweet
   That whenever a March-wind sighs
He sets the jewel-print of your feet
   In violets blue as your eyes,
To the woody hollows in which we meet
   And the valleys of Paradise.

The slender acacia would not shake
   One long milk-bloom on the tree;
The white lake-blossom fell into the lake
   As the pimpernel dozed on the lea;
But the rose was awake all night for
              your sake,
   Knowing your promise to me;
The lilies and roses were all awake,
   They sigh'd for the dawn and thee.

Queen rose of the rosebud garden of girls,
    Come hither, the dances are done,
In gloss of satin and glimmer of pearls,
    Queen lily and rose in one;
Shine out, little head, sunning over with curls,
    To the flowers, and be their sun.

There has fallen a splendid tear
    From the passion-flower at the gate.
She is coming, my dove, my dear;
    She is coming, my life, my fate;
The red rose cries, 'She is near, she is near';
    And the white rose weeps, 'She is late';
The larkspur listens, 'I hear, I hear';
    And the lily whispers, 'I wait'.

She is coming, my own, my sweet;
    Were it ever so airy a tread,
My heart would hear her and beat,
    Were it earth in an earthy bed;
My dust would hear her and beat,
    Had I lain for a century dead;
Would start and tremble under her feet,
    And blossom in purple and red.

Of all his poems, this one was peculiarly dear to Tennyson and remained so all his life. Although he denied that it was autobiographical, there are such striking similarities in the circumstances of the writer and his principal character, with their common background of tyrannical relations, frustrated love and the power of money, that it is generally believed that Tennyson was writing of his own experience. Only a small section of the poem is included here; the whole forms a work of great intensity with a tragic ending including lines as beautiful as any Tennyson wrote.

In the nineteenth century, before radio and television became part of everyone's life people made their own entertainment. At least one member of most families could play the piano and sing, thus creating a ready market for new songs. The Prince Consort was himself a successful composer and performer.

Many of Tennyson's poems were set to music and this is one from a song-cycle written for Sir Arthur Sullivan.

At the Window

Vine, vine and eglantine,
Clasp her window, trail and twine!
Rose, rose and clematis,
Trail and twine and clasp and kiss,
Kiss, kiss; and make her a bower
   All of flowers, and drop me a flower,
      Drop me a flower.

Vine, vine and eglantine,
Cannot a flower, a flower, be mine?
Rose, rose and clematis,
Drop me a flower, a flower, to kiss,
Kiss, kiss—and out of her bower
   All of flowers, a flower, a flower,
      Dropt, a flower.

Tennyson wrote some very amusing verse in the broad Lincolnshire dialect he remembered from his youth when he wandered the countryside talking to local people; it is interesting that in spite of his elevated position in society he never lost his Lincolnshire accent. Since one of his brothers became a curate and assisted their father at Somersby it is likely that this poem is based on fact. Seven verses are included.

The Church-Warden
and the Curate

Eн? good daäy! good daäy! thaw it
  bean't not mooch of a daäy,
Nasty, casselty weather! an' mea haäfe
  down wi' my haäy!

How be the farm gittin on? noäways.
  Gittin on i'deeäd!
Why, tonups was haäfe on 'em fingers
  an' toäs, an' the mare brokken-
  kneeäd,
An' pigs didn't sell at fall, an' wa lost
  wer Haldeny cow,
An' it beäts ma to knaw wot she died on,
  but wool's looking oop ony how.

An' soä they've maäde tha a parson, an'
  thou'll git along, niver fear,
Fur I beän chuch-warden mysen i' the
  parish fur fifteen year.
Well—sin ther beä chuch-wardens, ther
  mun be parsons an' all,
An' if t'ōne stick alongside t'uther the
  chuch weänt happen a fall.

Now I'll gie tha a bit o' my mind an'
    tha weant be taakin' offence,
Fur thou be a big scholard now wi' a
    hoonderd haäcre o' sense–
But sich an obstropulous lad–naay,
    naay–fur I minds tha sa well,
Tha'd niver not hopple thy tongue, an'
    the tongue's sit afire o' Hell,
As I says to my missis to-daay, when she
    hurl'd a plaäte at the cat
An' anoother ageän my noäse. Ya was
    niver sa bad as that.

But I minds when i' Howlaby beck won
    daäy ya was ticklin' o' trout,
An' keeäper'e seed ya an roon'd, an' 'e
    beal'd to ya 'Lad coom hout'
An' ya stood oop naäkt i' the beck, an'
    ya tell'd 'im to knaw his awn
    plaäce
An' ya call'd 'im a clown, ya did, an' ya
    thraw'd the fish i' 'is faäce,
An' 'e torn'd as red as a stag-tuckey's
    wattles, but theer an' then
I coämb'd 'im down, fur I promised ya'd
    niver not do it ageän.

An' I cotch'd tha wonst i' my garden,
  when thou was a height-year-
  howd,
An' I fun thy pockets as full o' my pip-
  pins as iver they'd 'owd,
An' thou was as peärky as owt, an' tha
  maäde me as mad as mad,
But I says to tha 'keeap 'em, an' welcome' fur thou was the Parson's
  lad.

An Parson 'e 'ears on it all, an' then
  taäkes kindly to me,
An' then I wur chose Chuch-warden an'
  coom'd to the top o' the tree,
Fur Quoloty's hall my friends, an' they
  maäkes ma a help to the poor,
When I gits the plaäte fuller o' Soondays
  nor ony chuch-warden afoor,
Fur if iver thy feyther'ed riled me I kep'
  mysen meeäk as a lamb,
An' saw by the Graäce o' the Lord, Mr.
  Harry, I ham wot I ham.

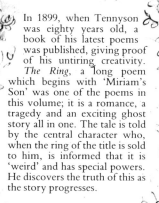

In 1899, when Tennyson
was eighty years old, a
book of his latest poems
was published, giving proof
of his untiring creativity.
The Ring, a long poem
which begins with 'Miriam's
Son' was one of the poems in
this volume; it is a romance, a
tragedy and an exciting ghost
story all in one. The tale is told
by the central character who,
when the ring of the title is sold
to him, is informed that it is
'weird' and has special powers.
He discovers the truth of this as
the story progresses.

Miriam's Song

MELLOW moon of heaven,
　Bright in blue,
Moon of married hearts,
　Hear me, you!

Twelve times in the year
　Bring me bliss,
Globing Honey Moons
　Bright as this.

Moon, you fade at times
　From the night.
Young again you grow
　Out of sight.

Silver crescent-curve,
　Coming soon,
Globe again, and make
　Honey Moon.

Shall not *my* love last,
　Moon, with you,
For ten thousand years
　Old and new?

The artistry with which Tennyson has conveyed the coming of spring in this poem, written in old age, can never cease to delight and astonish his readers. These are only two of the nine verses vividly describing the poet's feeling for the rebirth of nature after the icy grip of winter. Another poem, 'Early Spring', was written about this time and it, too, conjures up the Spirit of Spring for us in Tennyson's inimitable way.

The Progress of Spring

THE groundflame of the crocus breaks the mould,
    Fair Spring slides hither o'er the Southern sea,
Wavers on her thin stem the snowdrop cold
    That trembles not to kisses of the bee:
Come, Spring, for now from all the dripping eaves
    The spear of ice has wept itself away,
And hour by hour unfolding woodbine leaves
    O'er his uncertain shadow droops the day.

She comes! The loosen'd rivulets run;
    The frost-bead melts upon her golden hair;
Her mantle, slowly greening in the Sun,
    Now wraps her close, now arching leaves her bare
To breaths of balmier air;

Up leaps the lark, gone wild to welcome her,
    About her glance the tits, and shriek the jays,
Before her skims the jubilant woodpecker,
    The linnet's bosom blushes at her gaze,
While round her brows a woodland culver flits,
    Watching her large light eyes and gracious looks,
And in her open palm a halcyon sits
    Patient—the secret splendour of the brooks.
Come, Spring! She comes on waste and wood,
    On farm and field: but enter also here,
Diffuse thyself at will thro' all my blood,
    And, tho' thy violet sicken into sere,
Lodge with me all the year!

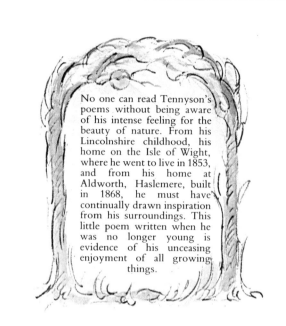

No one can read Tennyson's poems without being aware of his intense feeling for the beauty of nature. From his Lincolnshire childhood, his home on the Isle of Wight, where he went to live in 1853, and from his home at Aldworth, Haslemere, built in 1868, he must have continually drawn inspiration from his surroundings. This little poem written when he was no longer young is evidence of his unceasing enjoyment of all growing things.

The Snowdrop

MANY, many welcomes
February fair-maid,
Ever as of old time,
Solitary firstling,
Coming in the cold time,
Prophet of the gay time,
Prophet of the May time,
Prophet of the roses,
Many, many welcomes
February fair-maid!

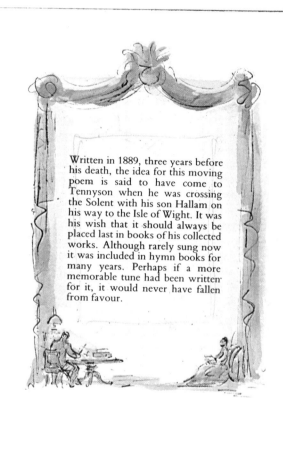

Written in 1889, three years before his death, the idea for this moving poem is said to have come to Tennyson when he was crossing the Solent with his son Hallam on his way to the Isle of Wight. It was his wish that it should always be placed last in books of his collected works. Although rarely sung now it was included in hymn books for many years. Perhaps if a more memorable tune had been written for it, it would never have fallen from favour.

Crossing the Bar

SUNSET and evening star,
  And one clear call for me!
And may there be no moaning of the bar,
  When I put out to sea,

But such a tide as moving seems asleep,
  Too full for sound and foam,
When that which drew from out the
        boundless deep
  Turns again home.

Twilight and evening bell,
  And after that the dark!
And may there be no sadness of farewell,
  When I embark;

For tho' from out our bourne of Time and
          Place
  The flood may bear me far,
I hope to see my Pilot face to face
  When I have crost the bar.